Changing

Changing Seasons

Edited by
Rebecca Mee

First published in Great Britain in 1998 by Poetry
Today, an imprint of
Penhaligon Page Ltd, 12 Godric Square, Maxwell Road,
Peterborough. PE2 7JJ

A Catalogue record for this book is available from the
British Library

ISBN 1 86226 501 1

Typesetting and layout, Penhaligon Page Ltd, England
Printed and bound by Forward Press Ltd, England

Foreword

Changing Seasons is a compilation of poetry, featuring some of our finest poets. The book gives an insight into the essence of modern living and deals with the reality of life today. We think we have created an anthology with a universal appeal.

There are many technical aspects to the writing of poetry and *Changing Seasons* contains free verse and examples of more structured work from a wealth of talented poets.

Poetry is a coat of many colours. Today's poets write in a limitless array of styles: traditional rhyming poetry is as alive and kicking today as modern free-verse. Language ranges from easily accessible to intricate and elusive.

Poems have a lot to offer in our fast-paced 'instant' world. Reading poems gives us an opportunity to sit back and explore ourselves and the world around us.

Contents

The Happy Butterfly

Creeping crawling all the day
Eating all that comes my way
Tasty, crunchy, lovely food
Keeps me in a happy mood
Feeling sleeping
Off I nod
Snoring loudly in my pod
When I wake one sunny day
I'll flap my wings and fly away

Jodie Saunders (7)

Turtles Hatching

At dusk, under Ascension sky
The lonely Frigate bird patrols his beat,
A silhouetted predator
With nature's dining-table 'neath his feet.

The early hatchling down below,
In fading daylight bids to cross the strand
Down to the sea, escape to make,
But with defences badly under-planned.

His undeveloped carapace
No armour 'gainst a frigate's piercing beak,
No company of brothers there
To shelter him, he is alone, the weak.

One swooping flight and he is gone,
Never to test the currents of the deep
That brought his mother back to this
Hereditary shore, whereon to weep

Her tears and strain to bury eggs.
The deep'ning darkness blurs the frigate's view
And homeward turns he, having supped
His last, while night airs cool the sand anew

And sensing so, the wise began
Their struggle to break free the earthbound nest,
Wherein for weeks they've gained their strength
To fit them fully for the seaborne quest

That faces, before they can return
This shore in search of cyclic parenthood.
What number will attain that goal?
How many, while still young, will lose life's blood?

The ferment stills. A head peeps out.
No moonlight yet and aerial threat declined,
As sand erupts four-score or more
Young turtles with their course to sea defined

By in-built knowledge of the risk
That waits, perhaps a prowling feral cat.
And fanning out, they tumbledown
The dune, seaward to where they were begat.

W A Wilkie

The Otter

As crisp dawn air envelopes the shimmering lake,
Something stirs in the undergrowth - a family of voles
With blind terror in their eyes, a hasty retreat they must make
From the deadly claws of the hawk - poor little souls.

The golden sun lazily appears above the low hilltop,
Butterflies adorn the nearby fields and trees,
Their delicate wings gleaming against the harvest crop -
Green, yellow, and orange, abundant beauty in the summer breeze.

One eye opens, then another - dawn awakes in sleepy hollow,
Velvety coat, dense to the touch - feeling weary and weak.
All curled up in a spartan, matted burrow
Of grasses and reeds - exquisite creature so sleek.

Otter, it haunts me that your fortune is untold,
With the mystery of a hazy future, we must not despair.
As I gaze here in awe, my thoughts will unfold -
A fearsome world surrounds us - nature has to take care.

Gliding so silently into the cool, misty water
With a shadow looming swiftly in the morning light,
At peace with yourself - not a lamb to the slaughter,
Subtle ripples are left - a lone survivor of the night.

Julie Bradford

Winter Birds

Robin jerked his way.
Barnacle Geese swam
Through the sharp lake of shining blue into
The pinking tinges of the orange
Sun.

Kings of tit abreast.
A thick band of dark
Swings in the stream
Of air, chancing
Nuts given by the chilled
Boy.

Before light reaches the depths
Of green and brown,
A white, ghostly, magical
Bird grabs its last frozen meal.
Small creatures dart and nestle
Amid warmth.

Standing, waiting on a wet bank,
Pointed beak, still as a solid icicle,
He bows his head onto the darting scales.
In a flash he has risen into the cool air
Drops of ice cover his smooth back
Forming unique crystals.

Lucy T Montgomery

Heron

The sun was pressing urgent shadows
across the lawn when I saw him,
silhouetted against marbled sky
looking for all the world like
he couldn't possibly fly.
A parabola on stilts that rose

awkwardly from the still waters held
mirror-like by lack of wind in
a thickly and soft-mossed stone basin
previously erected
in honour of some person
I would never meet but whose spoor told

all there was to know about her strife.
Lichened cherubs spat erratic
arcs which erupted in taut circles
on contact with the surface;
silvered moments like fickle
lovers in and out of her brief life.

Just in that one moment, legs warped by
meniscus, poised strangely fragile
between elements, his soul entered
hers, like a quiet ghost,
whereupon both were lifted
on the clear wings of the outstretched sky.

Gwyn Winter

Snails

Interesting monopods
With undulating undersides,
Have intricate embellishments
On spiralling establishments.
Their tentative eye tentacles
Trace parabolic silhouettes,
And suddenly extremities
Internally encapsulate.

Averyl Allen

Maisie

A swan on the river
Regal as a queen passed by
Then turned her fine head to the boy
Sitting alone on the bank

He fumbled for bread in a bag
It burst open, spilling crumbs
Upon the ripples: she nibbled at some
Then called him to her

They were together for a while.
She taught him in many ways -
Laughter and joy was theirs to share -
Till she laid him on the grass asleep

When he awoke she had passed on.
To where he did not know -
His heart pierced
Stopped was the world

In his hand he clasped a feather -
Its softness keeps him warm against the chill.
She swims ever on-in lakes and streams
You may see her-beautiful still

Gordon Rankin-Semple

8

Waiting For Godo - The Finale

Do not disturb that tabby cat
he dreams of no good thing
beneath a spiky temper lurks
a coiled and serpent spring

Do not disturb that scabby cat
oh thank God he is sleeping
a cannonball on one short fuse
and primed for detonating

Do not disturb that tabby cat
he's related to a tiger
a radioactive time bomb
a ticking Bengal Geiger

Do not disturb that scabby cat
he purrs before he strikes
green eyeballs of a grinning god
he does just what he likes

Do not disturb that tabby cat
pure poison's in his paws
a throwback to the Borgias
notice unsheathed claws

Do not disturb that scabby cat
he's not just any moggy
the bones are littered in our street
of many a poor stray doggie

Do not disturb that crabby cat
and pray for this poor sinner
I clean forgot his fishy treat
    . . . he'll wake up soon . . . for . . . dinner

   Des O'Donnell

Gull

Veering vision aloft
empyrean vessel
shot through with light.
All darkness doffed
a skeined coursing of the air
your flight,
buoyed by no hope
nor ballast shed
feathers bent into the wind
hold, lift, impel.

Wide sweep of eye
takes in without rejection
and mind lives only
to be borne thus.

Earth puts out wings and soars
a feathered thing
in your radiance.

Stan Radcliffe

Untitled

Reflections in a mirrored pool.
Effervescent colours shoot and arch,
In ever wondrous shapes and feelings.

Emotions run high in the jungle tonight.
As the panther stalks in the dappled
moonlight.

Its prey is unaware of impending doom
as it sleeps in perfect peace.

No sound.
Not a rustle.

Claws!

Razor sharp teeth glint and . . .
Snap!
Only for a moment . . .

Then a commotion ensues,
which soon dies and peace returns.

Leaving the blood to trickle down the river
and out to the open sea.

James Dyer

Nature's Acrobat

Little grey squirrel, so lithe and endearing,
Burying nuts in a bright, sunny clearing,
Diurnal forager of hedge and wood
Continually searching for his food.

His bushy tail of brownish grey,
Fringed with white of joyous ray.
With chestnut streak along his side
And limpid eyes full open wide.

Almond shaped giving wide angled vision,
Firmly fixed on his daily mission.
Soft twitching ears forever listening
And tiny nose ever moist and glistening.

His sense of smell, sharp and acute,
Ensures he'll find his hidden loot.
His delicate hand with fingers four,
Five on hind, but one less on fore.

So ideally suited for clutching his food;
Constantly in a receptive mood.
Cones, bark, nuts fruit and seeds,
Satisfy his gastronomic needs.

As days shorten his task grows harder
Searching for food to fill his larder.
Like a crow's nest, high in a tree,
A drey his home, for all to see.

He establishes a cache as a winter store,
But rarely remembers where he's hidden his score.
Relying on nose to locate his measure,
He invariably finds some of his treasure.

Nuts he's missed and failed to find
Will sprout and grow into their kind.
At camouflage he is the master,
But by stripping bark he causes disaster.

He's nature's acrobat, so graceful and agile;
Enchanting and delightful, but still full of guile.
The appealing look is sure to charm;
His enemy is man, who can do him harm.

The damage he does, he tries to make good
By burying seeds he regenerates the wood.

Bryan Colman Bird

Inmates

Caged, trapped, I feel ill at ease.
Frustration abounds, zoo keeper a tease.
I pace the same line
For the one thousandth time,
No hope of escape
Just cruel faces agape.

Excrement tickles, children they stare.
Some show me pity, respect for my lair.
Insanity kills me
Freak show curiosity,
I long to be home
To hunt, kill and roam.

Vacuous and dazed, resigned here to die.
No fight left within me, all limp here I lie.
Spirit so bruised
Scarred body abused,
I'm resigned to my fate;
For death I will wait.

Adrian James

Birdsong

There is a tree in blossom, in the grey
Maze of the city streets and shadowing walls.
Among the flowers, the soft winds gently sway,
Pale petals lightly falling. A bird calls
As if through sun-lit woodlands far away
Or high in the deep blue of cloudless day,
Free as the winds are free.
                                    O bird your cry
From earth's dark prison to that shining sky,
Tells of what sadness? The wide world in pain?
What sudden joy? How can you sing and sing?
How can your song, its piercing clear refrain,
Still echo so intensely such deep pain,
Such wild delight?
                                    The golden dawn along
The highest hills is yours; sundown on seas;
Low fields of summer flowers; cool shade of trees,
And valley streams: yours an immortal song.

And now within the silent city walls
It seems a voice from ancient forests cries,
From cataracts and mountain waterfalls
And unsailed oceans below sunset skies.

Small bird in the bright tree, you cannot know
Those things you sing, of lands so far away,
Of shores beyond blue seas, of endless day.
Yet to dim gardens and dark streets you bring
Your notes of silver, fair as any spring
That ever starred the grassy hills with flowers,
That ever washed the world in sparkling showers
And calmed the waves and made the rainbows glow.
Deep is the secret of the tune you sing
Like an old song, forgotten long ago.

Diana Momber

A Wondrous Sight

It was still dark over the lake,
The reeds swaying gently in a gathering breeze,
The cold water rippling slightly;
Everywhere was quiet, a deep, deep silence,
Eerie, sombre, untouched.
Then gradually the slow light of dawn
Began to show in the east,
And as the light commenced its journey
Over the surface of the lake,
The birds amongst the reeds started to stir,
And to shake their ruffled plumage.
Then just as my eyes had become accustomed to the light,
With a great swooshing and swirling,
Those beautiful creatures rose together as if by a signal,
From the grey of the water,
Up towards the light,
Onwards to the dawn,
Their great wings outstretched,
For an instant, shutting out the weak morning light,
And plunging me into darkness again.
Then with an echoing call,
And graceful flapping wings, they vanished from my sight,
And I was left with a joyous feeling of great elation
At that wondrous sight . . .

Sarah Fernandes

18

Dolphins

Such kindness I see
Between the dolphins and me,
Such gentle eyes and a gentle heart,
The dolphins and I shall never want to part.

So caring, such friends
But all good things have to have ends,
They'll always be there
In any problems they'll care.

They'll follow me wherever I go
Their my best friends, I hope they know,
They take me on rides over the sea
Just the dolphins and me.

I don't want to part
They will always be in my
Heart.

Louise Downing (10)

Moonlit Swan

A Blackbird sings in the clearing on a fence encircled by birchwood
Startled by the heavy plop of a frog that dives into the cool shallow
                                                    pond at his feet
He sings a warning of danger he has not seen

In the long tangled tufts of marshy grass stretching out before him
The quickening breath of a tiny fretful shrew whispers through the
                                                    air
Adding credence to the Blackbirds urgent plea
The cloak of night is no shelter against the hunters ghostly beak

The smell of moist earth fills the fading light
Alerting twitching fluffy nostrils hidden in green bracken on the rise
                                                    of a sandy hill
Lying close to the ground the rabbit senses fox
But he will not feed at this warren tonight

A distant river, the sound of running reel
A flashing trout has made a fine catch and will not see the morn
A swan rises noisily into the stilled evening air
Long droplets of moon silvered river sliding from his milken feathers
He will rest safe this night, upon a roman island nest beneath the
                                                    cold stone bridge

Dusk falls darker now, then into night
When the fisherman has gone home and the world is sleeping still
The Barn Owl, rare and beautiful, wild and free takes up his nightly
                                                    quest
Whilst the busy day light world gives way, to graceful peaceful rest

Catherine Greenup

The Weak Giant

Flexing the muscles
The mountains can be moved
With ease,
With eyes widely opened,
He jumps into the spider's
Warm welcoming arms,
The welcoming web,
His stomach is empty,
Into the bowl of the
Savoury pitcher-plant he lands
He is the antelope,
He runs with horns and gets caught
In thorns,
A trap,
The ant in the snoring elephant's
Nostrils,
The mighty mammal sleeps endlessly,
With the ant out and jubilating.

Kwadjo Attakora Baah

The Shire Mare

Beauty and power are wed
    In great engines.
Strength marries tenderness
    In the shire mare;
Sleek black voluptuous curves,
    Near motionless,
Embody patient calm
    Broken only
By tossing of her head.

Frail-legged, arch-necked, bright-eyed,
    Her foal stands by,
Impatient to be fed;
    Some milk escapes
And dribbles to the ground
    When the mare stirs,
Easing one mighty hoof,
    Gently from side to side.

Within this scene of sweet
    And placid love
The farrier works on;
    Blade cuts, file rasps
And pliers wrench dead flesh;
    Acid- sweet stench
Of searing heat as shoe
    Meets hoof; and then
The hammer's rhythmic beat.

The great beast never quails
    Since nails and fire
Touch only matter dead
    As a machine
In routine maintenance.
    So why is it
That to a looker-on
    Redemption speaks
Through driving in of nails?

Terence A Neal

Whales

Spy hopping in the shallow, calm waters that mirror every
       tree on the passing islands.
A large eye, peeping shyly at us, as we marvel at its grace.
       A clear cloud of spray billows into the air.
The mist left hanging above,
       like thousands of microscopic rhinestones.
Rays of soothing Canadian sun bask on its back,
       dappling and dancing over the strong skin.
While the whale balances on his tail, putting on his display,
       I wonder what it is to be beneath the straits,
Hearing the beautiful sound of his song,
       underwater, the song he communicates with,
With his friends, his children, tiny in comparison.
       We glide, side by side,
Our boat oddly like a steel mother for him,
       We glide, he follows us to Saltspring Island
As though to keep us safe.

Julia Elburn

Northern Dusk

In the long, soft evening
of a short northern summer
we sit by the cabin wall
the timber behind us still warm
from the sun.

I thought all would be greyness here,
desolate greyness under a low metal sky,
bleakness over permafrost.
And I see mountainsides ablaze
with golden lichen,
lifting the sky high above us,
glaciers groping their way
with vast exploring fingers
to the turquoise of the tarns,
the barren scree tempered
by the poppies' pale yellow,
the gorge speckled with the blue
of the silky willow.

The sun touches the white hood of the peak
then sinks away.
The shining summer clouds
are now a confusion of blurring shadows,
flickering, fading wisps of amber
die all around us.
The rolling call of the golden plover
'prre-quirrio prre-quirrio'
no longer drifts across the moors.

We sit in the deepening stillness
until the nascent moon appears,
a sickle in a field of stars.

Turid Houston

The Dragonfly

Two pairs of iridescenting
tender transparent wings
flutter towards her:
the little buzzing helicopter
intimates to land.

Four pairs of flimsy black legs
touch down tenderly
on the back of her hand.

One pair of glittering faceted eyes
peers into another pair of sad eyes
and she smiles.

Then she starts talking
to this very pretty little creature
by moving gently her head
from the right side
to the left side
and from the left side
to the right side again.

And the dragonfly answers
moving its very tiny little head
in a harmonious rhythm
with the movements of hers.

Half an hour lasts the ceremony
between them.
Then the dragonfly
sets off from her hand
waving Goodbye.

She suddenly starts to cry
so deeply touched
it feels
and she kneels down
to thank the celestials
for having sent her
a friend.

And she smiles again.

Sandra Ney

In Warm September Sea

Pacific dolphins toy with the bow
like snakes in a courtship frenzy,
or flames playing above an ember.
Sliding and gliding one over another
like the hands of a belly dancer
caressing the heady air about her.
And the white hull prances in accord
with the teasing slinky sirens smiling on.

E M Clifton

Invasion Of Privacy

Spider grimly wanders the wall
No-one cares at all
Freedom comes in different ways
Through your dreams, through the haze

Alistair Millar

The Old Horse

The old horse leans over the gate,
Children feed him and his mate.
He is glad of the peace, glad of the quiet,
Remembers the time he was caught in a riot.
The bomb that nearly ended his life,
Remembers the pain, the noise, the strife.
Got better with all the strength he could find
Funny - he'd always thought humans were kind.

Jose Segal

Summer Evening Lawns

August summer evenings balmy tranquillity pungent
fragrance lingering on the evening air.
Tall withes heavy with bloom white sprays nodding
sleepily.
Mallow pinks translucent magnificent 'gainst the
evening sun,
Looking down 'pon St John's Wort in aureate profusion,
an island in an emerald sea;
and each candied crimson lily cup glorious but for
a day shrinks before the silvery moon,
as night gives death to day.

K J Barrett

Summer Magic

What was that sound? I stepped from the path
And peered into the dark fastness of woodland.
I heard the faint chimes of a clock in a distant tower.
The evening shadows hid an army of creatures
Moving around me. The soft wing of a moth touched my face.
Then, in the still air, the stirrings ceased, the wood fell silent,
There was a strange excitement of anticipation,
As from a nearby bush came a plaintive cluster of notes,
An evocative call tossed in the air, a flow of melody
Piped as from a faery flute. The wood was bewitched
By the sound. Even the screech owls were silent.

The nightingale pursued his overture, trilling gently
As he composed the song for us. Short bursts of phrases
Interspersed with silences floated through the night air.
Then a brilliant cascade became a sparkling allegro,
A tumbling of notes from the very heart of the singer.
Immersed in the sound, I recalled the echoes
Of a vanished horizon, the world in the passion of its youth.
The song pouring from primeval woods into the new Millennium
Now upon us, the same sound, the offering of the bird
To its creator. A gift of love, indeed.

Lost in my thoughts in the beauty of the scene,
The litany of praise was fading into silence.
The woodland creatures resumed their nightly foraging,
I heard the soft brushing of feet and the harsh cry of a vixen.
In a daze I retraced my steps in the moonlight,
The clear plaintive notes still fresh in my ears.
A symphony of joy in the thrill of being alive
From a little brown bird on a sweet summer night.

Beryl Louise Penny

Blazing Sun

Sun blazing, a blue blanket for a background
Willow weeping as it bows to the triangular roofs
Sun pulsating with burning colour, flaring in the sky
Dark silhouettes standing erect as the warm,
radiating heat, of glaring rays dash through the houses
Blurring my vision as I admire the view

Lorraine Elizabeth Chaytor

Serenity

Sweeping shadows from the blue sky
Blend with summer's many colours,
Transforming them before the eye.

Evolving ever in our sight,
The strange unworldly beauty glows,
Dispensing jewels to delight.

Rendering all the gold and blue
Of the unclouded summer sky
A varied and more gentle hue.

Elusive visions rearrange
Their shape and form and density,
As light and darkness interchange.

No more substantial than the light,
Projected for the eye alone,
By rapidly approaching night.

Inset of bliss twixt night and day,
A sight, a taste, no more than this,
Too swiftly to be swept away.

Time of serenity and peace,
When day-time's manic pace is stilled,
And all too briefly troubles cease.

Yielding to night, its time is run.
Beauty in transit, setting sun.

Joan Isbister

Reflecting On A Drive Through The Trough Of Bowland

Where bluebells grow
Banks of green
Deep ravine
Streams below
Hungry hue
For my soul.

Heavenly blue
Periwinkle too
Eye and sea and sky
Blue
I love you

Elizabeth Leslie

Kora Eva

Lonely, the sea sobbed,
Heart, seaweed searching, unsought,
sighed.

Two rocks, rising, wave-wrapped,
were you, foam-felt,
you the lip-loved.

You
    were
        master music
            magic,
you the deathless.
Gothic, rising Godwards you were,
you the lifeless.
You were all; eternal Beauty,
you the ageless.

Lonely, the sea sobbed.

M Gubbins

Faces Of The Year

Spring's first morning, scintillating air
Earth's new growth with flowers in her hair
Young lambs leaping, frisking as they race
Thro' the meadows newly born,
That's her springtime face.

Sultry is the noontide, drowsy is the day
Bumble bees and butterflies pursue their painted way
Keen contented cattle, their verdant pastures pace
Awaiting even's solitude, behold her summer face.

Autumn evening, golden sky
Gilt-edged clouds that the wind throws by,
Pale blue vaults dressed in creamy lace
With fronds of gold, that's her autumn face.

Winter all encompassing, damp with mists and rain,
Diamond covered cobwebs deck the briars down the lane.
The watery sun tries valiantly the scudding clouds outpace
But all too soon 'tis dusk again, behold that's winter's face.

Norma Christina Robson

My Birthday

Let me not stay too long
Autumn has flurried by
And cold winter is come
With deceptive days of ease and sun, then
The iron door slams shut
And memories of hot, unhurried hours
Are pushed away into
Dusty corners, full of fading flowers.

Sheila Seabourne

Tree

Tree
Tall tree
Tough thick trunk
Travelling through time.

Karina Dingerkus

The Salmon Leaps Of Teifi

Fast falls the waters of Teifi
To tumble and flow
Over green moss stones
And salmon's brief show,
Into the calmer collected pools
Of blue cerulean glow
And shady nooks
Of the waiting streams below.

Finding for a while
The quiescent moments away,
And early evening's catch
Of soft whisperings of spray
That lie within the silver light
Of the river's deeper play,
Yet far beyond
The dark falls of rushing day.

Norman Royal

The Snow

When shall the snow go?
I cannot will,
When I see those three parts of myself
Those Lilliputians out there
Sliding, hurling, tumbling
In what is now my purgatory.
Each single diamond that glints,
Whether on bark or bough,
Hangs like a weight upon my soul.
At the waking flutter of the eyelids
It was there; the ceiling toned
To a new key, lit from below.
My heart sinks deeper - as the flood of consciousness
Absorbs the indelible fact of snow.
Yet, through the dark tunnel of memory
Vision reversing rushes to the bright day
When I would not learn, my eyes piercing,
Urging the classroom pane
To reel each jewelled morsel in.
The lesson lingered; the teacher's dreary drone
Evaded ears tuned only to the bell.
At last! That sudden clang
Shot me like a sprinter from the blocks
Out, out into the blinding light,
The soft shuffle of slithering shoes,
Criss-crossing snowballs - those ecstatic cries . . .
The vision fades. I am now old.
The anguish must remain.
That is why my refrain is still!
When shall the snow go?!
Why I cannot will.

W I D Scott

I Wished I Was A Wild Goose

I heard the wild geese call at evening
hauntingly, in salutation
and my heart was moved to melancholy
that I could not answer them.

I saw the wild geese fly at nightfall
silently, in high formation
and my spirits grieved in sad frustration
that I could not fly with them

I wished I was a wild goose.

Then in my dream the wild geese came
and took my hands and spoke my name
and I flew and called with them as one
and though my dream was quickly done -
my heart is glad, my spirit soothed.
I am dream brother to the wild goose.

Jean Collins

Shoreline

Smoothly up sloping sands the wave hisses
Softly on glistening pebbles the surf washes
Sensually around shy lips the breeze trembles
Suddenly in surging spray the sunlight flashes
Steeply down soaring cliffs the swift swoops
Sadly through creviced caves the swell sighs
Silently among staccato rocks the weed waves
Secretly within iridescent shells the past whispers
Ceaselessly from endless ages the sea calls . . .

Frank Casey

The Fallen

Across azure air above the grey
the thronging, duelling eagles chase.
A foe falls flayed from claws of steel
which shatter, mangle, maul and kill.

That stinging, ringing, withering hail
which rakes the skin from nose to tail,
with sudden, stunning, mortal clout,
sends them steeply spirraling from the rout.

Down from that wheeling, whirling fray
comes falling fast, the stricken prey.
A snarling arc across the sky,
ungainly flailing wings awry.

Pennon folded final against the sun,
toward destruction slips headlong.
Fractured, fiery fragments tinge red the gloom
that hide the earth and proffered doom.

A litany, long-since learned, on lips is heard,
as instruments, sight and thoughts grow blurred.
The patch-work world which whirls beneath
embracing all the clouds bequeath.

Frantic fists, unyielding frame,
The fight for life that dulls the pain.
Young sinews straining, muscles coiled.
The shame-filled sobs when clothes are soiled.

As one, enjoined in lasting scream,
is snuffed, impacted; made obscene.
Scattered, scorching, raging, the fiery flow,
atop the tomb that none will know. . . yet.

For those Airmen who are still 'Missing; believed killed'.

Dennis Martin

Line

A black green cormorant darts
too fast for the eye
as it flies low cosseted
in swaying waters.
Iridescent in death it dives
a bright scaled fish swallowed head first.
A scallop boat passes, swinging seaward
trailed by a flock of stuttering
gulls in benign courtship. Nearby
a congregation of preening birds pause
observe the shrill honk honking of hungry
children but ignore lean pickings.
Below, distanced, an isolate Fulmar stammers its wings
but once strained it glides rigid
and climbs imperceptibly.
This bird circles an arc
arms strummed in tune
starched and stencilled in
regimental markings it
dips and drops amongst
matronly gulls in acceptable flight.
Tip toeing its coverts
it zig zags a weave
and vanishes in breaking crests
and blue blown troughs;
funnels of the sea.
In passing, all too short.

Beyond, spray islets roll in grey waves.
In sheltered coves fettered rocks
wear wearily thin in an iron washed ocean whilst above
the Fulmar flies an unflappable line out to sea.

Tom Cunliffe

At Sunrise In The Park

The sun rising slowly in the chilly morning
sends pink and gold reflections throu' the semidark,
creating colourful contours in the sky,
silhouettes appearing on the skyline of the park.

White plumes of vapour stream and drift lazily across
the brightening sky, twisting, criss-crossing
and fluffing out into misty spirals
causing fancy patterns of nature's embossing.

Birds awakening from the trees flock noisily
circling, like black busy outlines above the trees;
the sky turns shades of increasing blue-pink hue
changing subtly, and clouds move gently on the early breeze.

As the great orb seems to move effortlessly upwards,
sparkly mosaics of frost show where early shadows were cast;
birds rummage hungrily for the early worm
as daylight arrives - another cycle, another dawn is past.

Ann Voaden

The Monarchs Of The Mountain

So having reached
your fine ancestral home.
Blossoming autumnal gold wings
upon the milkweed plants.
Bask in the warm haze of your
sequestered wintering ground.
Rest from wandering
proud monarch's in a
Mexican sun,
masquerading in masses
upon leaf laden boughs.
Blazing blizzards of butterflies,
shading light upon
your distant mountain.

Sheila Gartside

After The Gale

The wind's wild fury spent at last,
The land which crouched beneath
Its hammer blows
Lies in a bruised and battered daze.
Great splendid oaks
Which tottered, lurched and fell -
Their raw, pale flesh exposed -
Lie torn and shattered by the blast.

Beside the fence the leaves have piled
Like snow in drifts,
But now the sun which hid its face in terror
From rods of rain and thrashing hail,
Smiles briefly from a rifting sky.
A tiny wren goes mouselike through the thorn.
The brimming river, red with the lifeblood of the land
Swirls round the feet of willows bearing silvered wands,
And buds are swelling with a living green.
Now from a bush, a robin's trilling song
Proclaims, with hope,
That spring will not be long.

Mary Richards

Dutch Elm

Abject stands the once so friendly elm,
Stark against a blue and lively sky,
Reminding me of my mortality.
Among its shrivelled branches,
Only bats essay to fly,
While birds preen in the living trees,
Green, and stirring gently with the breeze
That lilts their leaves.
Soon the dry and sapless bark
Will crumble;
Roots will lose their hold.
The stricken trunk will tumble
To a dusty death,
In the summer Sun.

Walter Simkins

Sovereign Light

The moon, a yellow disc, hangs in a velvet sky,
And under it a silver sea laps gently on the beach.
A short, bright light flashing on a far, far reach,
The Sovereign Light winks by.
You're like that Sovereign Light that glows, then goes;
Your brightness fills my place then into darkness slides away.
Yet though our love more constant grows, day by day
You're still beyond my longing reach,
As is that light, far from the beach,
And I must content myself knowing that as the distant
         Sovereign Light
You will return, to make for me a few more hours bright.

R M Sadler

After High Tide

Sea weed
stranded on sand
shallow hammocks of green
mucous, sun-dried, fly infested
Seaweed.

Driftwood
twigs and branches,
bleached and twisted, bright sticks
strewn along the beach, tangled in
Seaweed.

Rock pools,
slate-grey bowls of
cold sea-brown consommé
garnished with slimy green tinsel
Seaweed.

Martyn McLennan

Beware Of The Sea

The sea so inviting
the sea so delighting
with cool silkiness
a caress on the skin
when you're done to a turn
(like a joint on a spit)
in the sun on the rocks
well oiled and so hot –

then beware of the sea –
beware of its chilly caress
because very soon
because in a while
the cool silkiness
may reach right inside
and the cold paralyse
to carry away
with the tide
and the current –

the sea so inviting
the sea so delighting
so green and so clear
with the bottom oh so
             deceptively
                 near . . .

Joanna Booth

Upland Nativity

It's Christmas day.
Sheep and shepherd have gone.
Sky a Madonna-blue

by the frozen tarn, no offerings
of voles and pipits.
Here, on a heather-clad spur,

the deserted merlin's nest
was a cradle in the rowan,
one star hinting at its presence.

Clyde Holmes

The Ocean

Haven't you noticed how I attract
you worthless creatures
of little brawn.

Who dare poison my world
and fill me with scorn.

No longer can I flow
so passively.
For you, my friends, are
annoying me.

My anger erupts like
whirls inside.
For all lost and for
those who died.

You think you can take
without a price,
and without a thought
of sacrifice.

So I grab my victims when I choose.
Gratification.
I've got nothing to lose.

I treasure my jewels
in beds of gold.
Hair flowing - secrets
never told.

I find so much comfort
from my little hoard.
When I touch and caress them
my warmth is restored.

But that, alas, begins to fade.
For the actions done
you haven't paid.

So I ask the winds to
Start a storm.
So you can learn what it's
like to mourn.

Deborah Krueger

Grass

From anguish flowers
the lily,
out of ecstasy
the rose,
in contentment
grass
for cow-cud grows.

Chris Moat

Wildflowers

waratah - where?
  here, and there.

wildflowers wild,
wily, windy more;
azure sky and crystal blue,
springtime blossoms, rainbow hues.

woodlands white and
turquoise bloom;
acacia rose
me to the moon.

wildflowers wild,
western lore;
kangaroo's paw, or
love galore?

linen loves, sorrow's silk;
virginity virtue chastity me.
Ours we share, what do they care?
We share wildflowers and wildflowers share we.

forever ever, never over;
others say, we clamour no way -

peculiar days,
wildflower days.

    Y F Leow

Creatures Ethereal And Bright

Surely our beloved summer-long companion,
The butterfly, gives us more pleasure
Than any other insect that beautifies or plagues
Our gardens, and adorns our leisure.

What a bumper season this has been for butterflies,
Particularly the handsome friend,
The Painted Lady, that migrant from the Continent,
Recognisable by their wing end.

In paler shades of orange than most of its fellows,
It resembles the Red Admirals,
With the white flecks on the wing tips, with the two fliers
Sometimes found together - insect pals!

Most spectacular of all our flitting visitors
Is the Peacock - its four eye-spots, blue,
Yellow surrounds, and dusky body; the small spotted
Queen of Spain Fritillary too.

The pretty little Meadow Brown has wings all darkened,
But bright eyes on a small orange mass -
On wing tips. The tiny Holly Blue - all true pale blue -
Must be quite our most delicate lass.

In shady lanes the Speckled Wood is seen - white speckled.
Black speckled is orange Tortoiseshell.
Dare we include, in this gay parade, the Cabbage White -
Which gardeners would consign to hell?

The Gatekeeper also has bright eyes on its wing tips,
The Comma's wings sharp and serrated.
What gardener has not been in his glory to observe
Butterflies on buddleias sated?

All these have been seen, in three seasons, in our garden -
One excepted - in North Worcestershire.
And all before, in an East Kent survey, in our field,
With the Skippers added in that shire.

And what a joy to find many of the same in Greece.
Creatures most ethereal and bright,
They catch our drowsy eyes on hot days, then rest at dusk,
When moths come out to fly to the light.

Jack Finch

A Great Respect For Worms!

Don't you look down on worms!
Squash me!
I have a great respect for worms.
We say: 'You worm, you make me squirm!
You're lower than the low.'
But worms make flowers grow!
They dig right down,
Dragging the debris of leaves with them.
Munching, crunching,
Squirming, turning their way,
Through mud.
Out of mud,
Grows Solomon's Seal,
And lilies.
Out of mud,
Grows wisdom.
When you're in the mud,
You have to get out.
Only a worm can tell you how!

Felicity Kaye

Alchemy

With each farewell a segment of us crumbles,
A well-loved water's-edge is washed away -
Enjambing, in alluvial alchemy,
The delta continuum of a yesterday.

Where willows comb their last blonde shafts of light,
What prow is it, lifting, senses the wind
And bears through the reeds, shadowy aboard?

Ah, do meet me there, by cedar vales of gold
Receiving recognition everywhere -
Not least because a errant elfin sigh
Blips circuitry twixt Us, Sun, Earth and Sky!

Karu-Anna Ramn-Menon

Cowslips

I walked one time upon a cowslip field,
And wondered how I saw this little flower -
Wide strewn in bonnet-yellow haze
Or singly as a fount of golden umbels
Oft kissing in the breeze
Like youthful lovers eager for a kiss?
And when in rain,
Sway and jig and cast their crystal drops
All ways around.
Or spatter some upon the emerald blades
As if to get them too, to join the dance.
I then began to muse
How such a tiny bloom of fluted hues
Can come, in scattered myriad mass,
To paint whole meadows in this tint,
And flame them yellow in the soft spring sun.
I trod with tender care
So not to crush one single little plant -
Lest doing so should taint
One millionth of this fragrant carpet.

Peter Wheatley

Spring Hymn

It's spring. It's spring!
It's sprung the spring!
I spring, I'm sprung!
Like tight coil my Soul bursts forth
As daffodils, crocus, cowslip
Burst with the first rays of the warm sun
Shocking the air with their scent
Trumpeting their presence
Swirling their shrill skirts in the breeze.

I'm shrill, I sing!
I join the birds in their lovemaking
Trill in their dawn chorus.
I'm woken by the amorous croaking of frogs
And my heart swells with all Creation.
Intoxicated, I too begin to build my nest
Driven by energy, joy, desire, primordial instinct

I strip the paper
Wash the walls
Paint the room
Sunshine yellow
Daffodil yellow
Spring yellow
Easter yellow

For This, All This
I thank you God.

Hermione Evans

The River

Amidst tall, snowy mountain peaks,
Born from earth's dark womb,
A crystal bubbling embryo springs,
River's life has quietly begun.

Emerging at first so softly,
Augmenting as it goes,
Waters surging upwards, joining,
The river as it flows.

Expanding its breadth it continues,
Passing a labyrinth of obstacles,
Winding its way ever downward,
Squeezing through narrowing gorges.

Forging through great rocky canyons,
Briskly boiling and rushing,
Foaming through the gates of hell,
Unpredictable rapids gushing.

Writhing as if in agony,
Over cataracts cascading,
Entering a peaceful stretch,
Turbulent soul reposing.

Gently, gently widening,
Banks wooed by progress milder,
Freed from its angry rage,
Pausing till the next chapter.

Swift and deep it marches on,
Running now with temperate sound,
Its journey almost done,
Destination homeward bound.

Banks wider and wider spreading,
Struggling currents flowing free,
The river's passage ending,
As it reaches open, roaming sea.

Janet Tinkler

Enchantment

There is a power in Nature with the strength to conquer Time:
It is older far than story, it is older far than rhyme;
It exists before the Ice Age and the rising of the Moon,
It extends into the Twilight and the furthest Crack of Doom;

It brings wisdom to the youthful heart, and vigour to the wise,
In the cruel depths of winter can bring clear summer skies;
It can ease the pangs of parting and can hasten the return,
Can bring comfort in the darkest night where lonely fires burn;

It is private in a crowded place, companion in the wild,
And grants to even weary eyes the vision of a child;
It is never found in commerce, to be bought for gold or lies,
Yet the whole of our existence would be worth so great a prize.

The Power? - It is a secret known to those, within its spell,
Who, when the spell is broken, are too desolate to tell.

Graham Waters

Early Morning
(This work is dedicated to my friend Suzanne)

Early morning,
one veiled voice.
Silent trees,
fellows of the lonely man.
Cry of seagulls,
uttering an everlasting sigh.

I,
the lovelorn,
looking at the Eternal Beauty;
Nature calls,
and I long for the rise
of pink clouds covering a black sun.
In a day-dream,
misty and mystical,
I raise my thoughts to the infinite ocean,
the Boundless Blueness,
till I'm lost in it.

And the seagulls uttered one more cry,
but of merriment.

F Sani

Untitled

Fulsome bloom.
       Womb of spring
Petal snow
Caress breeze tossed
Cares thrown
Burdens lost
       Blossom wealth.

Lavish hue
       Bluebell mist
Swaying haze
Of scented air
Hidden blaze
Mirage rare
       Of shimmering joy.

Relentless song
       Strong
With timeless energy
Lingering
Sweet agony
Bears spring
       Crie de coeur.

Like first love
       Moves
In an aura
Sun capsule
Cocoon warm
Nature's schedule
       Suffused with hope.

Gillian M Lowther

This Dazzling Land

Flowing down among crystal streams
　　　A sunlit river of boundless dreams
Under this sky so deep and blue
　　　I hear your voice come shining through
Reborn, my heart lays bare the scene
　　　A dazzling state of the in-between
Beset with doubts and dismal ghosts
　　　A longing light as the sunset goes . . .

Fires blaze beyond passion'd sight
　　　My spirit soars in enchanted night
Music swelling to fill the air
　　　The shadows that haunt no longer there
Jealous, still were the Gods on high
　　　In designs of malice - ate my mind
Betrayed by life, because they must
　　　Your image crumbled and blown to dust

Madness then reigned my weary soul
　　　As curtains fell over wanton hopes
Sorrow drowned upon barren land
　　　Eyes seared white by that burning Hand
Adrift, through storm you came to me
　　　A vision so strong, yet so needing
Belief in you was freedom from pain
　　　The tears came down as sparkling rain

Clive Froggatt

The Beach

Cold and windswept autumn beach
White horses racing.
In sight,
Yet out of reach.
Feel the spray, within the wind
Constant, but ending,
Yet to begin.
Like two young lovers,
Separate but one,
Holding hands before the sun.
And when the wind has gone
The horses leave
To graze pastures new,
With another breeze.
And so the lovers
Come and go,
Talk not of their parting,
For ours is not to know.
We can but guess
At what draws them close,
A sight, a sound,
A voice a breast.
And as the sun
Sinks slowly down,
The lovers leave
For another town.
The horses gone,
The sea is still
But with tomorrow,
Comes another thrill.

Hamish D Hamilton

The Sea

Impatiently
the angry sea
draws down to its depths
the helpless hand.

Its storms outlast
the granite shore;
turn cliff-tops
into sand.

Its drunken troughs and peaks,
the coward and the brave
still endure, endure and seek
an hour to rule the waves.

F J Shepherd

View From A Church Window

There's a thrill of blossom
On the old tree
A greeny-white chirrup of noise
Bouncing gently, like
A ball in child
Hands

Every nuance of creation
About the old tree
Tuned to perfection; you and me
Shaking our heads at confetti
Coming down like
Acid rain

A hymn to life
Such beauty!
Tiny waters of noise
Tongued lightly
At the kissing gate
Over there

Here, a dim view
Of immortality
As we pass our seasons by
Grown deaf
To each
Leaf

R N Taber

A Country Lane

The grass grows high in the rutted lane.
Rye grass. Cock's Foot and Yorkshire Fog
steal across the sun-dried mud,
to where the honeysuckle twines
tenderly, round the fallen log.
Along the hedge, the elders bow their heads.
And nod a creamy greeting to the clover,
sprawling, white and red, about their feet.
The lane is silent in the noonday heat.
Dreaming of sunset and the cooling night.
No hum of insects in the sun-dried grass.
No singing birds in bush or tree.
Only the soporific buzz of furry bumble bee,
deep in the purple-spotted foxglove bell.

Jess Chambers

Walking Home

Wading -
knee deep through
bright flashing waves of light
floating on clear water.

Below - a cushion
of algae softened stones
of many varied hues.

Sometimes -
bright green leaves
anchored but pointing
seawards, brightly flowing.

Darting -
stone coloured fish
glimpsed instantly they move
to camouflaged haven.

Sideways -
all sized crabs
run awkwardly for cover
from human feet
in
the estuary.

Pat Rees

One Day

Christmas calls one day a year
One day for peace and prayer.
One day to shed disharmony
One day to simply share.

One day to rest the wings of war
One day to wonder why.
One day to spend a moment
With the ones who need to cry.

To exercise compassion
In this cold and distant land
To love and feed the famined need
A warm protecting hand.

To sing this song of unity
To dance the dance of one.
To savour only happiness
When dissonance has gone.

I'm grateful baby Jesus
For this day of peaceful play.
But I'm sure you meant that Christmas time
Should fall on every day.

One day in three hundred plus
We celebrate your birth.
I hope you will be born again
One day on planet earth.

Patrick Tedman

Winter

It's the chilling air, chills the mind
It's the chilling wind, sweeps away hope
I walk in a misty morning, only to see nothing
Only to see, the maple tree, once red like a sweet dream
Now standing in vain
Vainly the birds have left for the warm south
Their home, now emptied mirth
Over the hill, beneath the dull canopy
Benumbed a naked wheatfield

In those days, there is nothing to see
In those days, there is nothing pretty to see
The sun, now on its remote course
Echoes a weak shine
Weakening even, rivers frozen
Snows fall

At night, when rough wind sweeps across the ocean silence
I make a cold dream

I wake up in the chilling dark
Thinking of tomorrow
Shall I keep in the cold
Or should I burn a fire
Should I believe cold days will pass
Wait until the warmth of spring
Wait until sun shines fine
Wait until warm days prevail

Wait until warm days prevail
I should believe time taking its course
That cold days come and go
And warm days follow, following the hardening season
  the spiritual father

Winter, in those cold days
There lives a warm hope

  Y Qin

Summer Dreams Of An Old Autumn

An autumn in an earlier decade;
A late evening, an old school -
                    house stove.
Memories . . . Seen from the heart
            And held in set eyes,
Like reflections in old windows;
Seeing out, and looking back to
            Rainy, Surrey skies.
The year seems fixed in autumn.
Here and away on scuffed dreams,
                    And boot polish.
Older doors bang, and echo.
Triangular faces fill out.

And some meaning is haunting,
When storm clouds were making;
The thunder and lightening,
And some voices breaking.

Scruffy is the past, and homely
As the scent of toast on autumn
                    Air.
So still, amidst the evening glow.
Tarnished bales of wheat, wine, and
                    'Cigarette sighs'.
Still an antiquarian, autumn mood.
Flushed in the moonlight,
And washed in wet, Surrey skies.

Michael-Francesco Paris

Leaves

The first spots of autumn on summers green,
sunlight dappled on the shimmering leaves,
one upon another, touching like lovers.

The sunlight bursts through,
a sparkling star,
a shaft so brilliant it illuminates all.

A gentle breeze flutters the leaves
like a flickering candle,
and a peaceful silence envelopes it all,
like a parcel for the one you love.

In the distance the hum of traffic,
the world goes on the same,
the moment's silence does not touch it.

And somewhere a tree falls,
comes crashing down,
another beauty gone,
and with the tree falls people's lives,
in floods, and fires, and wars.
But somewhere, somehow
is a shaft of light,
so brilliant it illuminates all,
and a tiny baby's cry.

Naomi Young

Seasons On The Thames At Reading

Awake no more my soul in joy at springs advancing blooms!
Suppress anticipation roused by knowing summer follows soon!
And from your mind's eye trained to welcome fare the warmer
season brings,
Erase those memories built up from former years of former things!

On Thameside reaches going west from Reading Bridge was often
seen
A maiden and her suitor chaperoned upon the upland bank of
green.
A boat or two would grace it all each moored beside the water's
side,
A swan with four young cygnets in procession through the ripples
glide.

On Thameside reaches going west beneath this modern summer sky
Among the litter, Ice-cream vans, a thousand people idly lie.
Boys and girls in shirt and jeans and many locked in rude embrace,
And houseboats in their hundreds now all occupying every space.

Awake my soul in joy at last now autumn's gold is here!
The jeans, the boys, the girls are gone. The avenues are clear.
At early dusk, on fallen leaves, through mist the autumn sun
descends
And leaves me to myself and to the vacant, settled, River Thames.

S P Alsop

A Christmas Forever

A Christmas journey was begun
when a bright green sprig of holly,
sprinkled with many deep red berries,
was nipped down and carried home by
three small rabbits. On their journey
their paws patterned their homeward path,
crossing the paths of birds and other
woodland creatures, across the snow covered
bed of the forest;
deep frozen icicles glistened in the cold
pale orange glow of the afternoon sun.

The tracks of foxes they crossed, and as the three
of them (two brothers and a sister) hopped silently
between each, each frozen twig, snow balanced
by nature's gravity, even the scent of the fox
told them not to fear as peace was at hand,
and that they could be their rabbit-selves

So into the burrow the three rabbits took their holly
and hung a beautiful bright green sprig of holly on
every rabbits' door. Underneath the hard frozen white
snow covered ground, in this warren of happiness the
rabbits evolved into adults, pheasants and partridges
into camouflaged shadows, the vixen with her pups
in her lair, jackdaws and crows sleeping deep
in the snow covered forest tree, relaxed.

The gentle glow of the now pale afternoon sun
kissed the snow covered top of the ploughed field
and threw her long twilight fingers into the slowly
deepening night of the Forest.

An Eternal peace came that night to the Forest, as an
unknown understanding of harmony grew between the different
animals of the Forest that special night.
And the presence of Christmas continues with all the occupants
of that Forest forever.

Rem Everett

Springtime

The warmth is creeping
through my soul.
My veins are pulsing
to be whole.
I sense with wonder
springtime's rhythm
a touch of sun
a breeze from heaven.

My spirit's mounting
to the trees
upward blowing
free, at ease.
My mind is clearing
with the skies
farewell to slumber
alert and wise.

My being rises
from the earth
pure white spirit
lightening birth.

A crystal ball
could not foresee
what springtime
feelings mean to me.

Frances Browne

Suite In Four Movements

Prelude (Spring)

Morning glory, early waking,
    Waiting for the sun to rise.
Pan, the little god of piping
    With the dew-mist in his eyes.
Innocent and bright with laughter,
    In this brave new time and place.
Unconcerned by what comes after,
    Childhood plays with careless grace.

Allegro (Summer)

Comes the time of wine and magic,
    Music played by candle shine.
Strange the heartache deeply tragic,
    Longing words cannot define.
Greedy, indiscreet, and reckless,
    Sweet the laughter, sad the tears.
Swift the sandals of quicksilver
    Running down the rainbow years.

Andante (Autumn)

Past the tumult of desiring,
    To a calmer, higher plane.
Now there comes with youths retiring
    Peace of mind serene and sane.
With the aftermath of sunset
    Comes a promise of repose.
Memories, as the long cadenza,
    Slowly draws toward a close.

Finale (Winter)

Age comes stealing as a nocturne,
   Played before the curfew rings.
Dimly from the land of shadows
   Steals the night on star-crossed wings.
Life, the whimsical musician
   Lays aside the final score,
And with exquisite precision breaks his pen -
   And writes no more.

   Elizabeth Stringer

The Tide

Spring. At equinox the tide turns.
Along the shoreline life re-kindles:
Gaudy lights re-lit, street stalls re-opened,
Shutters on the clubs and bingo halls taken down and locked away.
The people are returning;
A gentle breaker flowing across the promenade,
A more insistent surf; small crowds milling through the shops.
The sun rises earlier, sets later.
The beach takes the overspill from the pavements
And in pubs drinks are spilled.
The trains and coaches arrive full and leave empty.
At high summer the seafront is a frothing mass
The waves of people crash and boom across the esplanade
A deafening, endless noise
Before the evenings cool and the days follow
When coaches and trains arrive empty and leave full.
The tide ebbs slowly from the walk-ways
As the season dips towards autumn.
All is quiet. Hibernation once again.

Alan Clark

The Demise Of A Leaf

Fresh breezes of autumn have had their mad way
To carpet the forest in patchwork array.
Dry leaves of saffron, ruby and rust
Are fallen, withered and fading on pathway dust.
Sun in November, now milky and wan
Caresses bare branches, where squirrels leap and run.
While underneath, in decaying leaves
Beetles and bugs scoot below undressed trees.
This stretching sapling now bears just two leaves
As at top of the tree, to each other they cleave,
Jostled and blown, their playmates lost
Their hold, then see-sawed down in storm winds tossed.
But these two remain, defying separation,
Clinging to life, with mutual affection.
Together they struggle to stay that way,
As moon follows sun, as night follows day.

As one seemed to weaken, the other clung fast,
Then watched, broken hearted, as, victim at last
With withered form, and fragrance fading
One lost its hold, to earth cascading.
Dejected and lone, yet clinging to the tree
Hung the last leaf, in abject misery,
Until night came, then it fell too,
But greeting the dawn with wonderment new
As something almighty was happening now.
No longer a leaf at the whim of a bough
With kaleidoscope comrades, it merged with a force
In which all played a part in this great universe.
Each found new purpose, and seemed to be part
Of a plan, so tremendous! Death was simply the start.
Time they had dreaded, deprived of their tree
Now became heaven, they joined eternity.

Margaret Lawley

Christmas Cheer?

The sky went darkest black to North,
When all a sudden heavens broke forth
And poured out minions of fact
To proclaim the Earth's virginity intact.

The air filled with myriad hymns rejoice,
The canticles young and old in full voice,
The sweet perfume of minced pies baking,
The delicate aroma of mulled wine making.

The old wayfarer laid down his head,
Around no manger e'en for his bed,
Soon the deepest sleep he knew to fall,
Drunk on heady aroma of joy for all.

Two newspapers, one book a paltry bed,
Small comfort for one left alone for dead,
Sad, abandoned despite the festive cheer,
Praying for just one last swig of stale beer.

Remembered from so long ago he did sup
And toast old and young with festive cup,
Slowly, slowly he returns to beloved Beth,
Slowly, slowly he slipped to quiet death.

Paul Hetherington

Christmas Morning

A cold frosty morning
Box Hill a white ribbon.
O, come all ye faithful
Come to the priest.

> The pale sun at noonday
> Box Hill in white ermine.
> Fly home, merry gentlemen,
> Home to the feast.

> How swiftly at Christmas
> The cock on the steeple
> Swings from the celestial
> To the terrestrial.

Edward Murch

Night Song

At night when darkness like a velvet cloak comes down
And not a sound is heard beneath its muffled folds
Feelings, like a friend, become enhanced and grown
Proportion banished like the daylight bitter cold
Despair too near.

It's then our thoughts on roads untravelled make their way
To form unreal schemes and conjure up amazing dreams
Unbidden dreams, unwanted too, in light of day
When good propriety appears and truly seems
To calm our fear.

Patricia Stephenson

Migrating South

Blown by October breezes we stand under the brilliant sky,
Distance showing grey, carved from the blue, unmarred by cloud,
Not a sound, no bird, in sight until . . . there!
On the far horizon one infinite speck, moving swiftly
Followed by more, circling closer, still closer until
Immediately above, veering, swerving, swooping
These grand, white birds with giant great wings
Plummet down from overhead with known precision.
A gift endowed by nature
Yet far from the concept of man.

The meadow caught in meander - Quebec's great river,
Insignificant, its growing season passed
Grasses burnished from their green
And seeds, disturbed by breezes, drop at random.
These birds, these geese, know this so well
To return each fall in search of rest
To this same spot, transporting brown green ground
From quiet and peace to surging splendour
Of black tipped pinions, giant white wings
And guttural barks gargling from a garrulous gaggle.

Ensuing calm, for rest disturbingly acquired
With honking, more hooting and no time to lose.
Compelled to feed, feathers to preen, preparing
To circle south and fly from dark winter's grey-skied
Frozen grasp those thousand miles to find respite
On southern, sunny shores
With instinct so compelling, each bird aware of
Destiny, ignoring hazards unpredictable
From forces of storm, winds unnatural to steer off course
And helpless, struggling to escape fierce Nature's wrath.

Flying from beyond, momentarily poised,
The geese assess their chance to land with skill,
Silent, without disturbance, gently they swerve
To one selected spot.
We leave this field of smothered turbulence,
Barks hoots and honking now subside
As if a door were gently closed against the noise of crowded men.
The geese will fly rested and replete to leave
Their meadow now battered and deprived.
It has served them well and now, deserted, sombre,
Ready for snowbound sleep in winter's solitude.

E A Hackman

The End Of Autumn

Look dear, the world is at its best
As purple berries sway
Around the empty Blackbird's nest
Where gentle breezes play.
With finest golden trinkets
That sparkle in the sun
And glittering copper goblets
That brim full night and morn.

Listen the music comes sweetly
At first a single sound
A woodwind hidden completely,
The strings will soon respond
Drums echo round the valley,
Cymbals crash in the air
Brown leaves spin for one last dance
Then all is quiet and bare.

Sadly the flowers are over
Though fruits are full and fine
They are beautiful to gather,
Their wealth increased in wine.
So drink listen and wonder
Bask in the honeyed haze
The treasure and the memory
Will comfort darker days.

Juliet Dyson

Moonsong

Large and magnificent shone the moon
As it crept through a darkening sky.
Silvering its mercury touch on the world,
Burning cold, like a feverish eye.

It framed at first houses, then trees, then the spire
Of a church silhouette on the hill,
Then advanced with a purpose, an energy bright
In the dark sky, its silver to spill.

Chilly and blue, its light frosted the room
Softly swallowing colour and shape,
Tiptoed lightly and brightly, its footfalls all ice
And its influence hard to escape.

How boldly and proudly she now shows her face!
Little wonder it is that before
I return to the comfort of lullaby dreams,
I salute her with eyes full of awe.

Lianna Collins (20)

Tasting Bonfires

Bless the demise of sultry summer,
Blistering feet plunged deep into cascading streams,
Darting through cooling sprinkler spray on parched lawns
And splashing like children in paddling pools.
Celebrate the passing of lengthy,
Lazy days and heady, perfumed nights,
Lacy net curtains wandering in the breeze,
Chilled glass cider bottles on fiery foreheads,
Scent of coconut lotion in the mellow air,
Ringing telephones carrying lightly on the evening breath.
Bid farewell to delicate sunlight filtering
Through meshy blossom trees.
Dust floating in sunbeams, feasts of cherry strawberries
On the verge of new balmy days.
Instead receive the transition of bitter dawns,
Rusty leaves, coffee leaves, auburn leaves.
Embrace spicy scents, golden sundown's over toasted
Cornfields.
Tasting glossy blackberries, smooth blots on bramble
Landscapes.
Accept carved orange pumpkins,
Tawny thanks on excited Harvest festivals,
Smoky, burnished fires burning crisp in premature dusks,
Chestnut ash on scorched chocolate dust.
Relish the season of decay and magic,
When we dance, each as one, tasting bonfires.

Rebecca Williams

Feast!

A feast of sounds – the pure clarity of birdsong
A feast of colours – the hues of the autumn
Long shadows, and a yellow sunlight
From a low-slung sun
So the colours are enhanced
By the effect of halation

A feast in all senses
A freshness in the air
The active slowly letting slip
Its reins to the passive
An evening this evening
Frosts beckon
Tired more easily
It's just it's . . .

However, whatever – winter's dawning
A paradox I know
This feast carries us through
In our visual realm
A last flourishing stimulus
Before the bare bones ensue

But it needs to shed, it needs to be dark
It needs to be cold, it needs to be bare
The death enables . . . the life
The tree finds comfort in its roots
We must find comfort in passivity too–
A transitory transition
That makes flourishing possible
Savour the feast, but don't clutch it, or mimic it
It will be back, and it will be fresh
(And even the evergreens rest)

B Llewellyn

Spring

Sinks the sun beneath the distant haze
And hurries day towards predestined doom,
Its joyful colours fast submerged in gloom.
The ends of days?
So, winter too appears to play the king
Deceiving prostrate Nature he's the master of the earth
While She prepares in silence and in darkness her rebirth;
Comes on the spring!
So, with such powerful witnesses before our eyes
As morning every day and spring's repeated splendour,
How can we fail to grasp God's infinite agenda
And welcome that great spring when we ourselves shall rise?
Where is Death's sting? O, where indeed -
When buried lies the living seed?

Vaughan Stone

In A Philosophy Tutorial Assigning Words, Causes And Necessity

Another realm englassed,
posied irises purple streaked with white
stood from solar splendoured desk,
varnish jaded from other days.
Still as the window.

Outside, Sirius,
a drop in the zephyr stirred foliage;
this stars whited greens and blues incandescent,
reds and yellows prismed out tremulously.
The bright sky before eating time.

Bob Wilson

November Morning

Frail ghosts of bird songs
drift through spectered trees,
and hang upon the folds
of thickening fog;
with rain decaying
skeletal leaves that
mingling mud are
trodden underfoot.
And all is silence
through the muted world,
and high officials,
thwarted,
quietly fume over airport tea
and cars upon their
busy ways to nowhere
clog.
And all because of
nature's whim in
giving us a
morning, filled with fog.

Sarah Yeomans

Standing On The Sand

I got dizzy
When I looked at the skies,
I got scared when the raven saw my eyes,
I heard the sea-birds' returning cries,

And the sighs of the sea,
As it curled around me,
And my feet on the sand,
As I clung to the land,
And I feared I couldn't stand . . .

But only my skirt got wet,
And there was gladness I couldn't get
From any old place I was set.

Emily File

Winter's Intimate Stranger

The burst of a great frozen firework
Dazzling silver beneath the black December night
Suspended forever in memory and sight
Winter between us is the cold touch of the wind
Mirrors of frost on stone
Magic and pale words beautifully unspoken
A foolish desire to dance and sing
Make it summer with a kiss
Intimate stranger grant me this wish
It seems the scene was set to this time and place
With the mist of my breath I touched your face
Winter's intimate stranger
Will it always be December

Paul Andrew Jones

The Moon

the moon is in departure
and strikes her face to the sun
to flee upon a path of night
before she leaves my room

though not as old as time
she is wiser than the stars
and can see no future in their spin
around eternity

her glory gone
she is now all serenity and grace
her purpose of a higher state
as she encircles a silent Earth

R C Timothy

Christmas Week

Christmas week and bitter cold;
with carolled voices luminous
in frost-hung choirs:

exhaled epiphany . . .

a glimpse of nascent love
in brimfilled, ice-melt eyes,
too lachrymosely eager,

briefly burns
the willing frankincense and myrrh.

And then
like king or shepherd
we wait upon the pale new year again
and gently wipe away
our other, darker tears

Amen.

John Groves-Nation

Sonnet For Summer '96

The effervescent river, kissing sun,
Becomes a home in summer days so long.
In private gardens where showers are sung
By body impressed grass and leaves that turn
The mind to open space: the sunset sky
Invoking incandescent, feeling, touch
That brings from out of the ash the blood to rush
Towards the white sun, where the angels fly.

A softly swaying bed of clouds turn dark
And thunderous release explodes so that
Summer's heat is watered down to earth.

A shining stripe: the brooding, furrowed, parts;
The steam begins to rise. The sun attracts
The drenched: its rays embrace a well known hearth.

David Humphries

23 Degrees 27 Minutes

(This is the angle between Earth's axis and the plane of the ecliptic,
and is the basic cause of the seasons.)

Earth revolving on the year, its crystal kingdom melting
In the primacy of spring: under the willow's chandelier,
Glissando of the cool white swan of morning,
While the delicately rising river spills its tidal images
And floods the flat mind's fields with silver phrases.

Vertical in summer's noon, the golden watch
Of our celestial parent stops at Now
As if to prove resplendently without a shadow of doubt
That somewhere in the paradise of certainty enhanced
The heart of things is molten with delight.

Sunlight on its sapphire journey overtaking afternoon,
Begins to sing in crimson through the sadness of a park
Where the leaves are burning autumn in a festival of fire
While the evening people wander in a desert of regret
And the pleasure boats upon the water's lawn depend in sleep.

Darkness is arriving to prepare the way for children;
Another unborn universe is waiting for the Word;
The seeds of Time, descending into drifts of silence,
Winter through the empty quarter,
Safe in their remembering music.

Robert Gordon

Winter

Swirling snow
finds the glade,
hovers, lands,
turns to ice.
Adam's cold.

Soon his home
envelops
him with warmth.
Work is done,
time for rest.

Driving snow
fills the glade,
covers ferns,
clings to trees.
Silence reigns.

Winter's come.
Adam's glade
slumbers now.
Adam sleeps
forever.

Evelyn Golding

Summer Evening

When cool evening comes,
And scented flowers fill the air,
When long-fingered shadows
Lie upon the grass already dark with dew,
Then children sleep, nested like birds;
Hushed and still.
Softly the dusk falls:
Darkening the corners of the room
Till lighted lamps dispel
The melancholy gloom
And hold the night outside till dawn
When pale mists rise, and float away
As sunrise brings the glory of another day.

Olivia Barton

October Night 1987

Listen to the howling wind,
As it strips the forest bare.
Brutal, biting, bitter blast,
That freezes bones, rips at your hair.
Boiling up the oceans, running ships aground,
Causing havoc in the streets,
Hurling bins and slates around.
Rushing through the byways,
Using every means,
Crushing all resistance
Into smithereens.

Listen to the tempest,
As its anger goes unchecked.
Everything within its grasp
Is torn to shreds and wrecked.
The Gods whip on its fury
Raining down a billion lashes,
And goad it with electric darts
In million-volt bright flashes.
It rampages, demented,
Through each placid state,
No-one abroad can last the night
Before its wrath and hate.

Listen to the raging storm,
Whining through the rows and eaves.
While we cower in the warm
It's smashing sheds, uprooting trees.
Lurching like some drunkard
Over field and farm,
Until it tires and drifts away,
Then morning comes,
And calm.

Frank McKeown

The Thunder Of A Train

Summertime meant:
a bushel and a half of live crabs
steamed in domestic beer and apple cider vinegar
of warm watermelon, soft French ice-cream, fudge pudding, and
                                                    peanut brittle,
of rock candy, Scotch kisses, kosher pickles, and mustard greens,
of navy beans, ginger beer and ginger pop.

Summertime meant:
Papa Obi and Uncle Laney
spreading the Sunday newspaper on the back porch
as if it is a tablecloth made of fine linen or China silk.
All in preparation for a family feast.

Aunt Muffy and her four babes
Aunt Nee and her three
Papa Obi, Uncle Laney, and me.

Suddenly
the thunder of a distant train intrudes upon our only enjoyment
the thunder of a nearby train suddenly stops to collect our past and
                                                    our tomorrow.
Suddenly
the thunder of a passing train fades into the dying night.

Linda James

Warm Summer Nights

The sky is set ablaze,
Once azure,
Now the burning fiery colours of a flame.
The trees have become ripe,
Bearing the precious seeds of nature,
So sumptuous, so alive.
A cool breeze sweeps through the atmosphere,
Possessing the gentle fragrance of flourishing roses.
In the air is the warmth of the summer nights,
Carved in the meadows,
The silhouettes of the beauteous worldly sights.
The luminary light is summoned and drained,
Sunk into the darkness,
Only to be reborn again.

Reena Mandalia

Winter Journey

Stabbed breath, knife cold
That catches movement in an arch of ice,
And polishes glass in a field.

Where sheep bleat
A hunger underfrosted in the grass,
And mist misery
In a heavy cloud
Of carbon monoxide,
Deathly and too austere.

The beauty keens
Uncompromising,
Too brittle for a sun
That hides its slushing, its spoil
In a lemon sash
Of pretty deceit.

The white ruin is a mirage
Of another light,
That has no place here.
Here, where time runs out,
And food must soften,
And life must taint.

Ros Wass

Frame Of Reference

Our zimmer frames prop forward step by step
while suppler movers sheathe themselves in cars
      and stereo pap.
Our cosy homes are pulled about our ears
      and duvets cuddle us to sleep.

Our towns are proofed with bars of blatant neon
which blind our scrutiny of the aching sky
      our search for Zion.
We floss ourselves in arch photography
      build patios to barbecue on.

Maps used to scroll a reassuring border
of heaven's floor and ranks of angel hosts
      and God kept order.
But our delusions breed materialists
      who focus only through camcorders.

We tap a message to a virtual friend
and talk to mobile phones for status.
      We watch the trend
and regulate our bodies' apparatus.
      We dare not face the sun unscreened.

Michael Thurlow

Deadlines

In a new state of nature, red and brown
And black road absorbing the seeping heat of life
Lay the fox in a final quiver

Wildness bordered the tarmac
And the ley lines of pylons traced new sources of power
Over the old ways

This was once a safe route
Thick in autumns muddy trails
With the print of passing life

In minutes the relics of the fox
Are forever bound in the common elements
Of rubber and tar

Held for a modern eternity
Of moments
Carried forward, forgotten

Where is the wildwood away from the jungle
Where savage nature
Is a compassionate release.

Nathaniel Houston

Dusk

The sun has long dipped behind the fells,
And waves of pink cloud
Faded to a pale decrescendo,
Dusk settles,
Enveloping the river-bank in mystery;
Drifting scents,
Released from moist leaf and petal,
Hold the air;
With slow majesty, the moon lifts
Over the rim of the earth,
Lining the horizon
With a silvery phosphorescence,
Swinging low over field and meadow,
Seeking the dark liquid pools
Of the silver-flecked river, where
Among reeds and rushes,
A playful wind dances to the murmur
Of its soothing pianissimo.
Enchantment,
Dipped in the flickering shadows of night,
Soon to melt
In the glowing arms of Aurora,
    Fading out
        like a dream.

Pam Ramage

Winter Into Spring

The old, dark, mottled oak tree
stretches out lacy, bare limbs,
to touch cool sunlight, a radiance skittering
and glittering a promise of renascence.
From stark branches nesting birds
open wide their beaks
to cry loud mating songs -
impatient at the call to generation.
And the listening green-eyed overfed black cat
claiming the territory of the garden, acts out stalking
and hunting, crouching low and pouncing
on dead leaves carried by the wind . . .
Over the trees' wide trunk, clamber busy
sharp-eyed squirrels, scrambling up and down
round and round in a chase,
broad, furry tails outstretched.
At the trees foot green tips of growing bulbs appear
pushing up through heavy black earth
and perpetual night, into bright light.
And nearby, the cold ice on the pond has cracked
and thawed at last, now water ripples
to the dreams of soon-to-wake frogs
cosseted in the mud beneath.
Spring will soon be here.

Sheila Lahr

Summer Lingers

Summer lingers
In the glow of autumn light,
Summer trails,
And longs to stay as bright
As ever it was,
In the months just gone.

Fading colours,
Lighter than the garish hues
Summer brought,
Show her that she must lose,
For autumn is here,
And she should now go.

Summer lingers,
While still thinking, I suppose,
Autumn prime
Will not encroach, and close
Upon the beauty
Summer created.

Margaret Godfrey

Jam

Black berry
make merry
for winter.

Xandra Gilchrist

Old Father Autumn

Old Father Autumn bows his head
The time has come for trees to shed
Their leafy palms, and winter's fruit
Till spring endows an emerald suit.
For dainty blooms to snuggle and sleep
In shrouded games, of hide-and-seek
While cousins hardy, defiant stand
And brave the ravages, at hand,
For autumn's triumph, proud and free
Paints pastel shades on bush and tree
Hue of orange, red and browns
A mixed kaleidoscope abounds.
Till winter sounds its mystic chant
Submissions bow, by tree and plant
For those who frisk and scurry about
To rest in sleep, till winter's out.
And those, who fly to warmer skies
To flee with novice, young and wise
On beating wings of grace and haste
While winter rambles, free to taste
The still and calm, of autumn's sleep
Till winter's wandering is complete.
And spring - from Mother Earth bestirs
In cascade blooms and dancing birds
The fanfare call, that heralds spring
A mass return, on beating wing
Of colours picked flamboyant, loud
As swaying, ocean fields endowed
With life's own spark and kindred flame
The beauty, zest - not one can tame.

P Ashby

White Christmas

Fresh, cold and wet.
Gleaming at daybreak.
Camouflaging the land.
Brightness hurts my eyes.
Sleigh marks engraved on the hillside,
Evidence of children playing.
Icicles glisten like diamonds
Soon to disappear.

Warmth of the fire fills the room,
Surrendering to the aroma of the Turkey Roast.
Fairy lights glow on the tree,
Multi-coloured paper, new presents
Litter the carpet.
The cacophony of voices
Echoes in my ears.

B M Ellis

Christmas Morning

In the perpetual beauty of early dawn
all I have longed for
all the love that died
and empty places in my soul where hide
little sparks of hope
lighten perceptibly for we can cope
with only so much sorrow in a day
unable still to drink eternity
to break our will

And now the days are short
dawn comes late
liquid clear
lighting the winter wood
lifting again the heavy cloud of night
from meadow trees
the gently sloping lawn
and huddled dumpling sheep beyond the gate
touching their fleece with silver

So they stood
when shepherds saw a light
and felt a nameless surge of hope
dissolving nameless fear
pointing a way

Beyond the beauty of a dawning day
I hear the christchild crying in a manger.

Anne Stevens

Summer Is A-Coming

Cernunos dies, the Stag of nature
consumed by the winter's cold blasting winds
perishes even as the leaves of trees
fall and creatures sleep, so the Great Horned God
dies as the light of day grows shorter day
by autumn day until all nature sleeps.
There Cernunos sleeps for winter has come.
But as the Great God rises so the Green Man
in Him breaks forth in the livery of spring,
for summer is a-coming, He'll not stay dead.

Break forth Cernunos, Cern Giant break forth
from winter's grip; tear out the old growth
with your antlers O Mighty God of spring.
Rise up summer from winter's cold roots:
off with your dark mantle, shake off your death.
O Cernunos and most mighty Helidd,
you of vigorous frame, rise from the Earth,
regenerate your abundance of green forms.

Teasers of the Green Man, young virile maids,
here is Cernunos to make you fruitful.
Beg His pleasure, retreat in bashfulness:
lead the Horned God on, avoid His touch.
Oh beautiful young woman give your lips
so full and seeking, your arms all rounded,
your white breasts and waiting thighs a quiver
and knees and calves and ankles that make quick
the eyes of men: give give give and take take.
But you are the fickle teaser of the God,
knowing He follows where you are going.

The procession moves on.

John Jarrett

123

A Dawn

The grey dawn, with low clouds
Sea mist floating over the sands
To merge and join within the valley.
The mist, wet and cold
Clinging to the beard,
Lank hair thrown back
No sun, the wind freshens.

Slowly as the day starts
The sun warms
Struggling to burn away
The morning mists.
No warmth as yet,
Comfort taken from the
Few rays of mist laden light
That manage to pierce
The leaden gloom.

One ray, two
Reach the welcome earth.
A gentle streaming
As dew drops evaporate
Into the morning light.
The warming land awakes,
Refreshed and gladdened
As the world awakes.
The grasses take a hue
Of many greens, flowers
Of every colour open in joy,
And over the fire the kettle
Sings in unison with the dawn.

Robin Colville

Seasons Meetings

Memories of winter seem inviting in the dusty sunlight
                                        of August,
Coolness in lungs and freshness on faces contrasts
                                        with warm-jacket-must.
I want this for a time, until it arrives.
Constant heated shoulders and damp skin,
Garage sale of body parts little used, kept in.
Once flush with annual redness,
Limbs vanish with the advent of long evening recesses.
Four-PM - darkness hides skin that's un-necessary,
What's left becomes flush with the redness of January.

'The grass is always greener',
Say those without desire,
Waiting for seasons changes to near,
Complaining to the fire.

If I keep cold in mind,
Heat is bearable, fragile,
I savour its beat and endure.
If I keep heat in mind,
Cold is cleaner, less tangible,
I endure its cut, anticipate its cure.

Dan Brown

Darkness And Delight. An Ode To Winter

Feathered wisps of breath upon the air
Are drawn in tingling gasps from my bosom's heart,
And in suspended animation without care,
Like wraiths of mist they whisper on the breeze.

Liquid sunlight trickles through gaps between the trees.
Melting into molten rivulets of gold,
And mingling with the leaves of bronze like debris,
Scattered freely on the whim of a wind.

Violet, pink and white rose blossoms settle,
As floating garlands overhead
Swirling mixtures of fragrant petals
Clouds reflecting nature's winter bloom.

Mighty oak and beech and chestnut
Silhouette on lemon grey,
Layers and levels heralding
The ending of another day.

Silver bladed cloud cleft sun
In copper kettle raiment clothed,
Wears a smile, a cloak of benevolence
Wrapped around the sky,
And beset with pearls and jewels,
Glistens as it dies.

Moon and stars shine crisp and brilliant,
Fairy lanterns strung up high,
Shimmering against the sunset
Telling us that winter's nigh.

Liz Pamment

Christmas Lights

christmas lights

shimmer now over
unsteady lives, re
move

peering dusk for
arid cards with perplexities -
yearning to

follow eyes down
under (guilt
never looked for) - to
divulge pain;

but do they
underestimate how
yellow

their shine is; i d
ream of
impassive soul-searchers
phasing by

and coaxing this
radiance through the window's
dreary

(nothing)

   Scott Docherty

Harvest

Soft Pebbles
Like the whites of eye,
Blind the eye,
Ignored by sheep.

Marshmallow
Spawned in dung
Smooth as maiden's skin,
While underneath,
Women's folds
Damp and dark
Remain a mystery
Until the turning.

Chiaroscuro
Plaint in the even light,
Fragile, eager,
Weightless
In his greedy hand.

Sally Spedding

Winter In The City

Silhouettes of small birds
cling to sparse skeletal trees
like tattered leaves.

The suddenness of night,
dark, without the gentleness of dusk.
And burnt by sullen glare of city lights
the hurt sky cannot rest.

No winter evensong
from this paved wilderness,
save the unending drone
of distant traffic going home.

While we suburban slumberers
gaze dully at computer screen
and measure life from nine to five.
Unheeding of the patient cycle of the year,
the unseen life beneath the aching ground.

Sylvia Eden

Natural Springs

Friends journey from far and wide
finding centres where they eat and buy,
in towns and places on energy lines
if they need to replace, recharging life.
Exchanging, borrowing, flying kites,
soon days become shorter with longer nights,
leaves fall and squirrels hide
rusty colours blow day and night.
A festival lights up the skies
a celebration of all our lives,
the new year brings another tide
good things bad things, all in time.
Getting together to heat the days
by talking, doing, feeling ways,
twinkling stars in cosmic skies
friends with drinks at firesides.
Thunder, snow, lightning, rain,
seen every year but never the same.
Sharing the birth of another new spring,
sowing the seeds, growing within.
Looking on colours and hearing new sounds
the latest tricks and the coolest styles,
pebbles washed up at ocean's shore
fruits from trees on garden's floor,
birds sing with spirit and warmth
and carry the light, yes, natural springs forth.

Matt Seigne

Easter

So we come to that time of year
When we give thanks for your sacrifice
As we pray in the vigil in the chapel all night
We remember the agony of your plight.

In the Garden of Gethsemene
About to be betrayed
On your own, disciples all gone
As you pondered on what was to come.

The Sanhedrim took you away that night
Everyone knew the moment had come
But now alone with only your thoughts
We remember the miracles that you performed.

Now all alone, your disciples all gone
We look to your memory to cleanse our souls
Forgiveness you preached despite what they did
From Judas to Calvary you transfigured my faith.

P Telling

What A Lovely . . . I

I'm a ragged amputee.
I bleed; profuse, glutinous;
Weeping wounds sear;
Limbs hang heavy, hideous,
Yet tremble with fear.
Now, the Transients transport me,
To a claustrophobic, stenching, skyless place:
No kindred spirit here; nothing lives free.
Must I die slowly, alone in disgrace?
Rather, a dignified death:
Let lightning's fiery flash fell me sheer,
And free my fragrant arboreal breath.
They shake me now, and slash and leer,
Group closer and adorn in scorn.
Twisting, vain vines burn, with raw rainbow light:
Surreal, sinister fruits, suspend sharply by thorn:
Crumpled, shrouded creatures; dead offerings, are laid beneath.
With whom do Transients tryst?
I am dying now: dehydration.
Listen! That sound! A sacringbell? Can I become well; free?
And what is this weird incantation?
It's incomprehensible to me:
'What a lovely Christmas Tree!'

Sam Gannon

Flotsam And Jetsam

A scrappy cormorant with ragged wings
Dives in an empty sea.
Little boys stand disconsolate
With loose, slack lines.
An old man scours the shore
Amidst cracked, empty shells,
Relics of mussel beds,
Maritime graveyard.

Where once shimmering porpoises danced
Rain dripping from proud brows.
Basking sharks sliced through sea
Eagerly escorting in boats filled
To the gunnels with silver backed catch.
A shine of seals poised to somersault
Beneath the bubbles, shower of spray
Above a sudden shoal.

A solitary heron stands idly scanning sky
Keening seagulls swoop in close from shore.
Coots and mallards share a frugal meal
With a bedraggled white swan.
Oyster catchers scavenge at the water's edge
Pecking through the thin, limp strands
Amidst man's burial mounds of rotting refuse,
Which cannot sustain them.

Heather Bruyère Watt

Motoralgia

Cars, cars, cars scars,
Count their number, count the stars,
Over the heel,
The wheel
Takes man with easy speed
To carry out each mundane deed.

No weary legs or breathless rush;
These days he never has to push,
He can listen, he can talk;
God help him if he has to walk.
If ahead the traffic's dead
What will he do for daily bread?

Pass the time
With gin and lime?
Look at the sky
With a bleary eye
And wonder what that 'green' is,
More likely where the screen is?

The 'Countryside' what's that?
Daren't go out without a hat.
Needs a road sign and an AA route,
Can't travel far without a boot,
For the pushchair and the shopping
'Out of Town' and back without stopping.

Near of not he'll take the car,
Without him it won't go far.
Without 'it' he just won't go,
The road afoot he doesn't know.
The road ahead he doesn't see,
Obese and unaware is he.

Jack Lowe

Tranquillity

Naked
Skinny
Tall
Crooked.
They own the land.

Sadly many have been sculpted
By human hands.
Oh I see one not quite naked.
Its generous arms reach
To all the corners of the earth.

A shadow casts upon it.
The train moves on.
They don't look
As glorious now.

A shadow has walked across the land
And taken away the colours of the world.

Joe-Anne Angus